I can draw

I can draw

COVENT
GARDEN
BOOKS

COVENT
GARDEN
BOOKS

Designed by Penny Lamprell
Illustrated by Jenny Williams
& the Peter Bull Art Studio
Written and edited by
Lorrie Mack
US Editor Margaret Parrish
Photography by Andy Crawford

Senior Editor Ros Walford
DTP designer Kavita Varma
Associate Publisher Nigel Duffield
Consultant Emma Drew

First published in Great Britain in 2010
First American edition in 2010

Published in the United States by
DK Publishing Inc
375 Hudson Street
New York, New York 10014
Copyright © 2010 Dorling Kindersley
Limited, London

Contains material from *I Can Draw Animals*
(2006), *I Can Draw Dinosaurs (2006)*,
I Can Draw Machines (2006), *I Can Draw*
Magical Creatures (2006)

ISBN 978-0-7566-7328-4

Color reproduction by ICON and Media
Development & Printing Ltd,
United Kingdom.
Printed and bound in China by Hung Hing.

Contents

Dinosaurs

Machines

I can draw
Animals

Animal stuff

COLLECT LOTS OF DIFFERENT artists' materials so your drawings can be as varied as possible. When you have time, experiment with all your pens and pencils to discover new effects you can create.

charcoal stick

eraser

use an eraser or a finger to smudge charcoal like this

soft pencil, for shading

No. 2 pencil for outline

sketch pad

pencil

colored paper

colored pencils

soft pastels are powdery and smudgeable— good for soft shadows and blending

oil pastels are greasy and a bit hard to blend— use them for rough textures like elephant skin

Something to follow

From magazines, cut out pictures of all the animals you want to draw and keep them for reference. Stuffed animals can show you how your creatures look in 3-D, and odd feathers will help you to get your bird wings and tails just right.

cut-out photographs

feathers

felt-tip pens

toy animals

ballpoint pen

watercolor pencil and paint brush

Animal gallery

FOLLOW OUR STEP-BY-STEP instructions for drawing lots of animals like the ones shown here. Start with a fluffy chick and you'll soon be working on a huge jungle elephant!

Owl

Pony

Piglet

Frog

Puppies

Bear cubs

Elephant

Duckling

Duckling

Lamb

Mouse

Kittens

Hen and chicks

13

Rabbit

Frog

ribbit

Chick

Close-ups

ANIMALS have the same kind of face as you—with a mouth, a nose, two eyes, and two ears—but each one looks completely different.

Piglet

Bear cub

Parrot

Arrange big circles and small ones to make a basic shape.

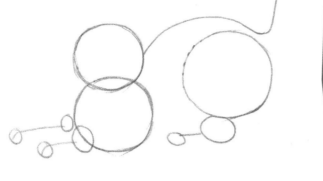

Link all the circles with curved lines to form your outline.

Kitten

KITTENS LOVE TO PLAY. They have sharp claws that tangle yarn and long, curly tails they can chase. To keep their fur clean, they lick their paws and rub it.

Draw the ears and fill in her mouth, nose, and eyes.

Add finishing touches like whiskers and shaded fur.

Use lines of shading on the kitten's body to suggest her warm, soft coat.

Draw a fat oval for the body, and circles for the thighs and head. Use straight lines for the ears and legs.

Make an outline that links and rounds out all the shapes you have drawn.

Rabbit

RABBITS HAVE LONG, FLOPPY ears and a short fluffy tail. Their favorite foods are green, leafy plants that grow in farmers' fields and people's backyards.

3 Fill in details on the ears, the paws, and the face—and add whiskers!

Use shading to make your bunny's fur look silky, soft, and warm.

1

As well as circles, you'll need ovals and a rectangle to start your drawing off.

2

Join the shapes to form an outline, rounding out the legs at the same time.

3

Now give your puppy toes, long ears, and a black nose that can smell trouble.

Puppy

With his floppy ears and big eyes, this puppy looks very innocent, but don't be fooled—he's looking for mischief!

woof! woof!

Your puppy could have a fluffy, hairy coat or a smooth one with lots of spots.

Odds and ends

WE CAN SPOT A FEW ANIMALS by one unique part of their body: an elephant's trunk, for example, or a pig's snout. But creatures that are very different sometimes have similar features—like kittens' and puppies' paws, or the wings on a parrot and an owl.

Puppy

Ear, ear

Rabbit

Kitten

Piglet

Wonderful wings

Owl

Parrot

22

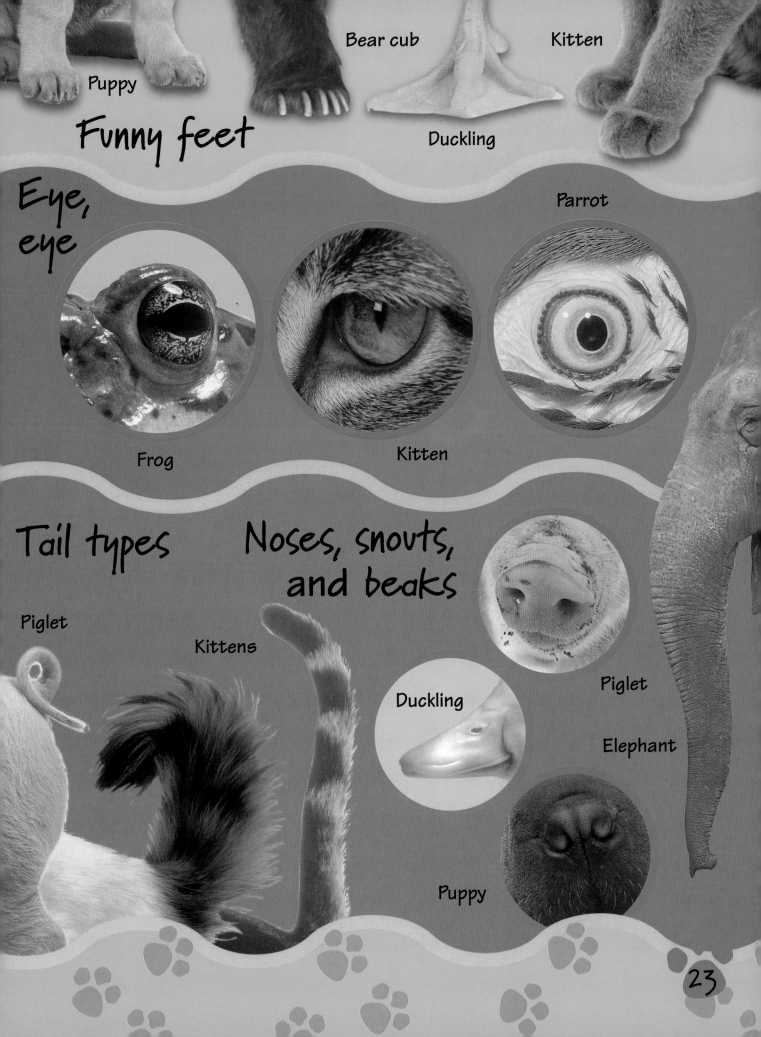

Funny feet

Puppy

Bear cub

Kitten

Duckling

Eye, eye

Parrot

Frog

Kitten

Tail types

Noses, snouts, and beaks

Piglet

Kittens

Duckling

Piglet

Elephant

Puppy

23

Chick

BABY CHICKS PECK their way out of their mother's eggs. The tiny newborns are yellow with soft, fluffy feathers.

1 Overlap circles to make rough shapes for the head and body.

cheep! cheep!

Fill in the textures on his feet and feathers.

2 Add a few linking curves to form your outline.

3 Draw details of his face, wings, and tail.

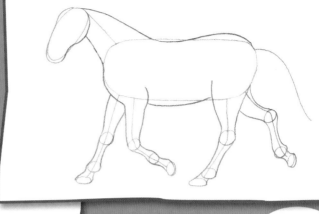

1 Start with sausage shapes, then add lines for the neck and tail, and lines and circles for the legs.

2 Draw an outline of the pony's body by linking the shapes.

Pony

DRAW YOUR VERY own pony so you can dream about grooming him and taking him out for long rides.

3 Fill in the tail, the mane, the forelock, and the ears.

4 Add details on his face and hooves, and texture on his mane and tail.

Shading makes his face and dappled coat more lifelike.

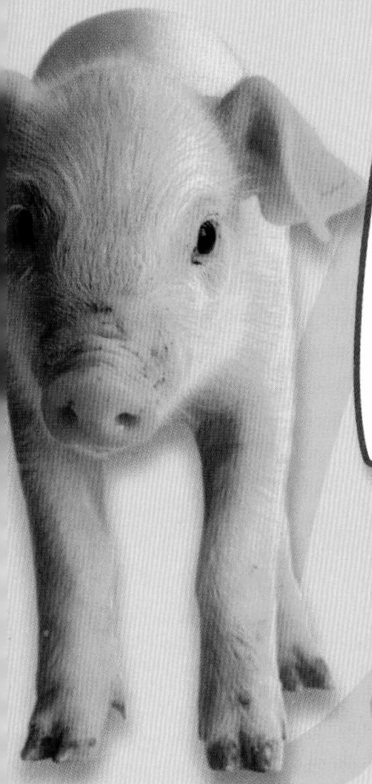

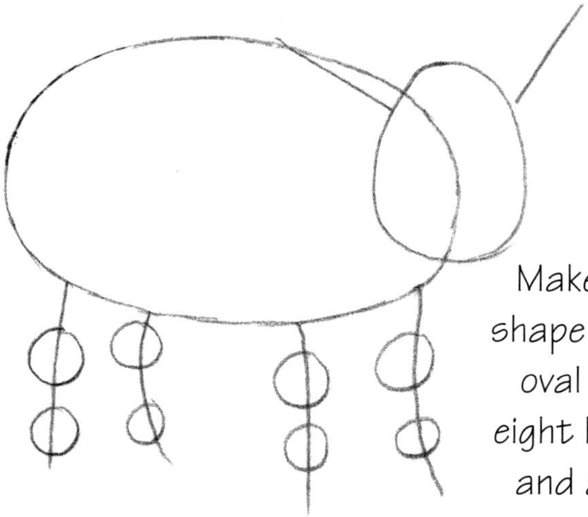

Make the basic shape with one big oval and circle, eight little circles, and a few lines.

2

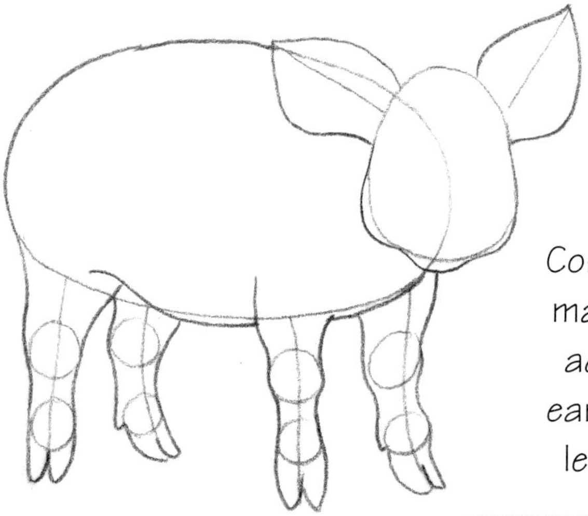

Connect them to make an outline, adding hooves, ears, and chubby legs as you go.

3

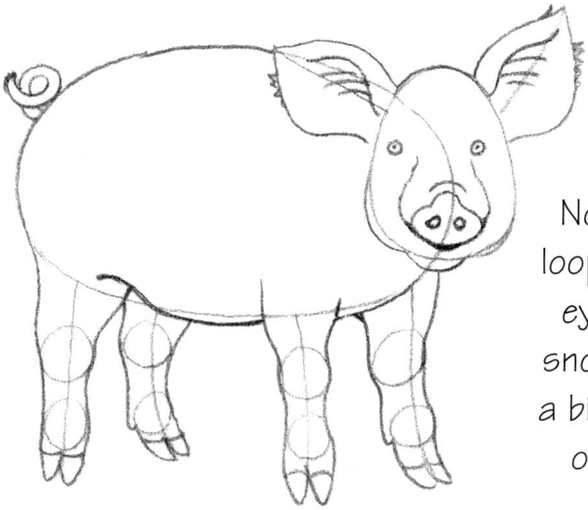

Now draw his loopy tail, piggy eyes, and big snout, and add a bit of shading on his ears.

Soft shading makes his legs and body look round and realistic.

Piglet

oink !
oink !

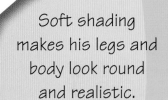

LIKE GROWN-UP PIGS, babies use their wide, flat snouts to sniff for food in the ground. They keep bugs off their skin by rolling around in the mud.

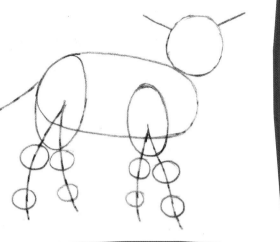

1 Start with circles, sausage shapes, and a few lines.

2 Join your shapes to make the outline, then add mouth, ears, and hooves.

Lamb

LITTLE LAMBS live in big groups called herds with their families and friends. When they grow up, their thick coats will be cut off and made into wool.

3 Put details on his face, suggest wool with squiggles, and add some grass.

baa baa!

Use lots of tiny curls and circles for texture.

No. 2 pencil, for general outline

soft pencil, for shading

colored pencil, for soft color

felt-tip pen, for strong color

Shading

Use DIFFERENT KINDS of shading to make your animals look more exciting and real.

Try out different pens and pencils to get the effects you want.

ribbit, ribbit!

pastel, for soft color

charcoal stick, for soft edges

eraser, for smudging

Types of shading

Diagonal lines will add depth to your drawing. For darker shading, make them closer together.

For crosshatching, make lots of straight lines, then add more lines going the other way.

Stippling is using lots of tiny dots to create different levels of shading.

The secret's in the shading.

Details that count

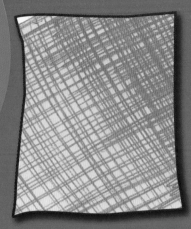

See how flat and dull the piglet above looks compared to the tubby, lifelike one on the right. What a difference some shade makes!

1 Start with a small teardrop shape and a large one, then add circles and lines for his legs, tail, and ears.

2 Draw your outline. Fill in his legs and feet, his smooth tube-shaped tail, and his ears, mouth, and nose.

3 Add eyes, long whiskers, and a bit of fur around the edges.

Mouse

IS THERE A MOUSE in your house? Maybe—house mice live all over the world, except in the Arctic and the Antarctic.

Use your shading skills to make his fur coat look thick and soft.

1. Draw a sausage-shaped body that narrows at one end. Add circles and sticks for the head and legs, more circles for the ears, and curved lines for the muzzle.

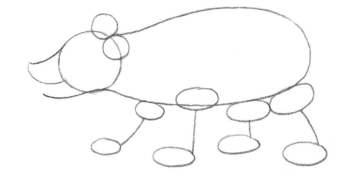

2. Round out the body and legs, adding a gentle bump on your cub's back. Now use your eraser to make some of your basic shapes less obvious.

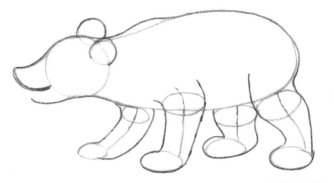

3. Fill in the detail on his face, ears, and claws, then use small jagged scribbly lines to indicate his rough fur.

Bear cub

BABY BEARS ARE BORN blind and bald, but after a few months, they can see, they have a furry coat, and they like to play together.

growl, growl!

Texture will make your cub's coat lifelike.

Frog

HAPPY TO LIVE in water or on land, frogs have long, strong back legs so they can jump very far and very high.

1 Arrange two eyelike shapes for the frog's body. Add circles for his eyes, and ovals and lines for his legs.

2 Link the shapes to form your outline, then round out the legs and add three webbed feet.

Shading works just as well for
showing smooth shiny skin as it
does for suggesting fur.

3 Fill in the eyes, mouth, and nose,
and draw the last webbed foot and
the small bump on his back.

4 Start giving your frog's skin some
color and texture, and add a pale
stripe down his back.

1 Start with lots of circles and a few curved lines.

2 Draw an outline around the shapes, adding a pointed tail and beak, plus legs and feet.

3 Fill in your duckling's eye, beak, and wing, and ruffle up a few of his feathers!

Duckling

DUCKS ARE VERY SMART birds—
they can fly *and* they can swim.
Even the babies have soft, oily feathers
that keep them warm and dry inside.

Use lots of short, light strokes to fill in your duckling's waterproof feathers.

Texture

USE YOUR NEW SKILLS and all your artists' materials to add depth and texture to the animals you draw.

I'm all lumpy and knobbly.

You'll find me in the trees.

I have long hair AND short hair.

I can tickle you with these.

My fur is soft and cuddly.

I need thick, hard skin.

Texture tips

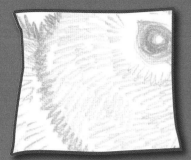

Show the soft fur on kittens and rabbits with light, smudged lines.

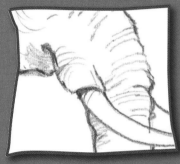

Tough pig or elephant hide needs thick, strong texture marks.

Bring feathers to life using long delicate strokes filled in with short soft ones.

Words to think about

scaly furry
bumpy lumpy
smooth slimy hairy
prickly spiky
feathery shiny

I'm very furry —I need soft edges.

1 Use circles, a cone, two sideways teardrops, and a few lines to make your basic owl shape.

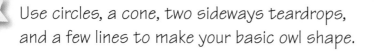

2 Join the shapes to make an outline, then draw the claws and face, and a few wing and tail feathers.

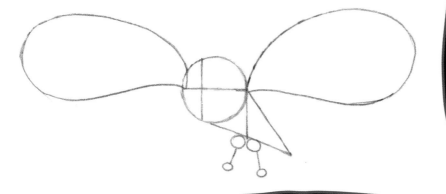

3 Take time to sketch in lots of curvy, graceful feathers on your owl's wings and tail.

A little soft shading brings your owl's face, body, and wings magically to life.

Owl

Tuwhit tuwhoo!
Barn owls have
sweet heart-shaped faces,
but they are fierce hunters
who eat rats and mice.

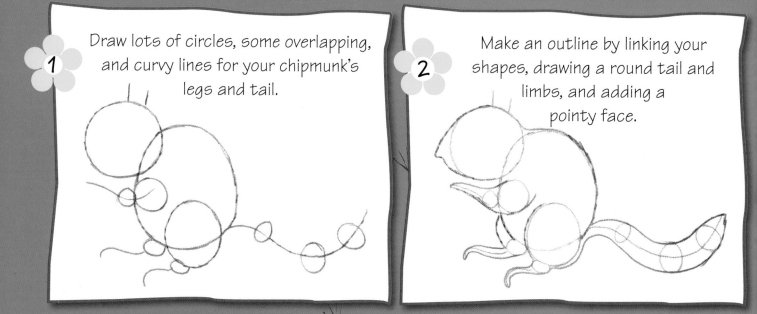

1
Draw lots of circles, some overlapping, and curvy lines for your chipmunk's legs and tail.

2
Make an outline by linking your shapes, drawing a round tail and limbs, and adding a pointy face.

Chipmunk

WHEN THEY FIND yummy nuts and seeds to eat, chipmunks carry them home inside their pouchy cheeks.

3 Add ears, a tiny eye, and claws that look like hands and feet.

4 Now draw whiskers and use shading to suggest a stripey coat.

Use lots of short lines to provide texture that fades from dark to light. This creates the impression of fur.

Parrot

AT HOME IN STEAMY jungles, parrots are very, very noisy, with sharp bills and lots of bright feathers.

1

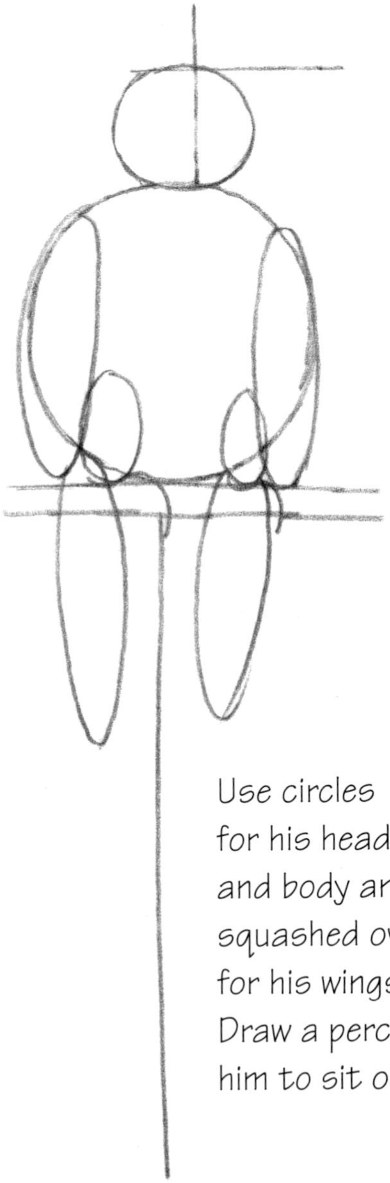

Use circles
for his head
and body and
squashed ovals
for his wings.
Draw a perch for
him to sit on.

2

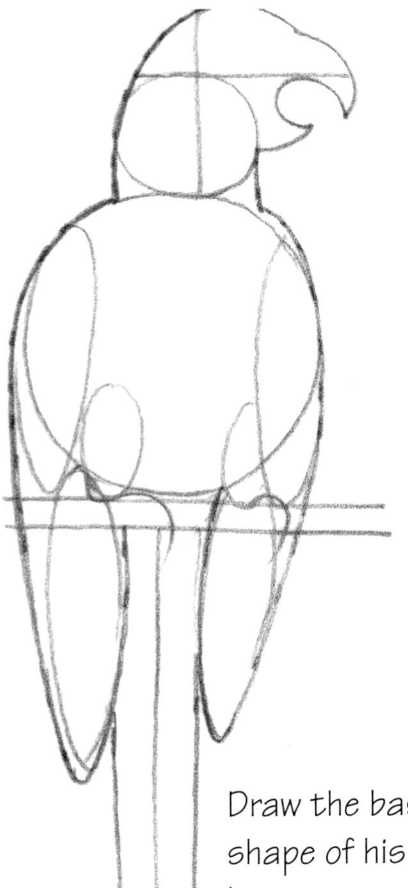

Draw the basic
shape of his
long
tail feathers and
his hooked
beak.

Add sharp claws around the perch, a beady eye, and more detailing on all his feathers.

Squawk! Squawk!

Use short, soft lines to give texture to his claws, his feathers, his beak, and his wooden perch.

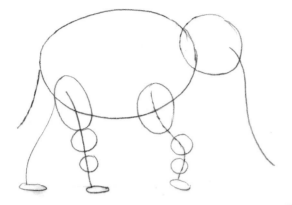

1 Use circles and ovals for the head, body, and legs, and long lines for the trunk and tail.

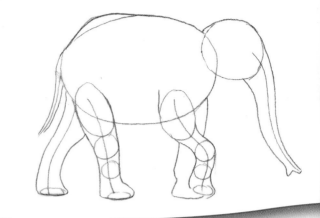

2 Shape the legs and feet, then the body, trunk, and tail.

Elephant

THIS HUGE BEAST has a long trunk to smell, eat, and drink with, and enormous ears that he uses like giant fans to cool himself down.

3 Add big floppy ears, pointed tusks, toes, and a paintbrushy tip to the tail.

4 Fill in your elephant's eye and start to add texture to his skin.

Bring his rough, thick, bumpy skin to life with subtle shading.

Scale

SOME ANIMALS, LIKE MICE, chicks, and frogs, are so tiny you could hold one in your hand. But adult elephants and ponies are MUCH bigger than you!

Sensible sizes

If you draw more than one animal on the page, try to make sure they're all roughly the right size in relation to each other. A big mouse would look silly next to a tiny bear!

Near or far

When you're drawing a whole picture, remember that the closer objects are to the front, the bigger they should be.

Woof!

Baby elephants are bigger than grown-up dogs!

53

I can draw DINOSAURS

Dinosaur stuff

ARTISTS USE ALL KINDS OF OBJECTS for ideas on what to draw. Get the effects of different textures with the materials below. Have fun looking for things to give you inspiration!

water-soluble color pencils

paintbrush

colored pencils

eraser

pencil sharpener

Color in a drawing with water-soluble colored pencils. Use a wet paintbrush to soften the color.

charcoal

soft drawing pencil

Draw in your sketch pad... try out all the dinosaurs in this book

No. 2 pencil

felt-tip pens

oil pastels

Sketch pads can be fun too!

Use construction paper.

Collect some cones, feathers, and shells to compare their textures.

Cut out pictures from magazines and newspapers to help you with your drawings.

Look at plastic dinosaur toys to see different shapes.

Dinosaur gallery

DINOSAURS ROAMED THE EARTH for over 150 million years. Bring them back to life with your pencils, pastels, and felt-tip pens.

Diplodocus

Triceratops

Euoplocephalus

Corythosaurus

Hypsilophodon

Lesothosaurus

Archaeopteryx

Compsognathus

Tyrannosaurus rex

Iguanodon

Stegosaurus

59

Tyrannosaurus rex

Styracosaurus

Velociraptor

Head to head

THE NAME DINOSAUR MEANS "GREAT LIZARD." Each dinosaur had different features to help it survive. Meet dinosaurs of all shapes, colors, and sizes.

Hypsilophodon

Troodon

Compsognathus

Edmontonia

Stegoceras

Compsognathus

Velociraptor

Suchomimus

Corythosaurus

Archaeopteryx

Iguanodon

Lesothosaurus

61

Grrr!

1 A single line gives you the spine of the dinosaur. Add circles to create the head, body, and legs.

2 Draw around the circles to shape the dinosaur's outline.

3 Now add details, such as the toes, teeth, and eyes. Erase the circles to finish your drawing.

T. rex

GRRRR! My name is T (Tyrannosaurus rex), one of the fiercest dinosaurs that ever stalked the Earth. I have big teeth as long as knives. Draw me at your peril!

1 Draw a curved line for the main shape of the dinosaur. Add lines and circles for its head and legs.

2 Draw the body outline and give your dinosaur two more legs and an eye.

3 Continue to put more details onto your drawing until you get a finished picture. Use shading to give your dinosaur scaly skin.

Triceratops

MY NECK IS SHORT AND THICK to hold up my heavy head. You'd better behave or I'll come at you with my horns!

Grrrr!

1 First draw a line for the body shape. Use a small circle to create the head and larger circles for the main parts of the body.

2 Draw an outline around the dinosaur to get the body shape.

3 Draw plates on the top of the dinosaur's back and add more details to its body.

66

Stegosaurus

I LIKE TO EAT PLANTS. My beak is sharp so I can bite off yummy green leaves. I protect myself from attackers with my sharp, spiked tail. How well can you draw me?

Wow!

Textures

HAVE FUN BRINGING OUT DIFFERENT TEXTURES on your dinosaur drawings using pencils, pastels, and felt-tip pens.

Re-create colors, shapes, and patterns on different dinosaurs' skin.

Triceratops

Corythosaurus

Stegosaurus

Compare the dinosaur on the right with the one on the left, and see how adding shading and texture has created a much more lifelike look.

Types of Textures

Draw thicker lines and stronger outlines with a soft pencil. Textures can make the dinosaur look 3-D.

Use charcoal or a soft pencil to show textures on a dinosaur's skin and bones.

To get the effect of scaly skin use a soft pencil for shading.

Aaark! Give me some depth, man.

Words to get you going

smooth feathers

shadows depth

sharp teeth

wrinkly skin

eyeballs shiny

scales lumpy deep

scratches

1 Use a line for the main length of the body. The tail will be as long as the neck and body.

2 Draw around the circles to get the shape of the dinosaur.

3 Give your dinosaur some claws and an eye.

Gallimimus

I HAVE A REALLY LONG NECK AND MY EYES ARE VERY BIG. I can swivel my head to see things in different directions. I feed on insects, plants, and lizards. Look how long my tail is!

Make the dinosaur's skin look scaly with shading.

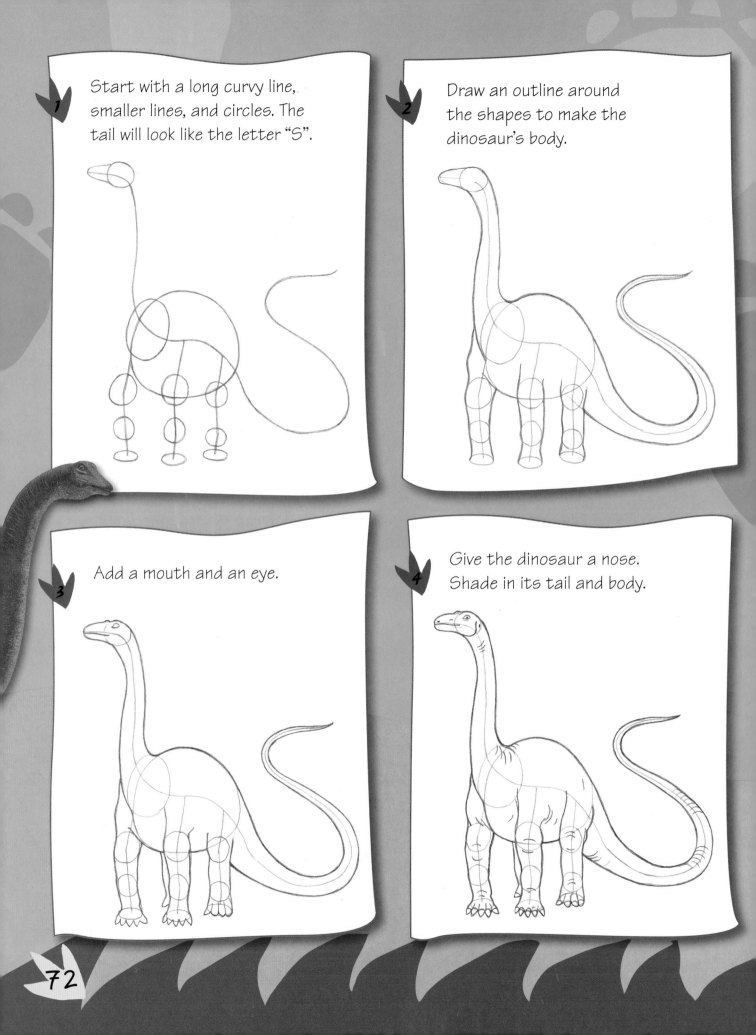

1 Start with a long curvy line, smaller lines, and circles. The tail will look like the letter "S".

2 Draw an outline around the shapes to make the dinosaur's body.

3 Add a mouth and an eye.

4 Give the dinosaur a nose. Shade in its tail and body.

I say!

Diplodocus

I HAVE THE LONGEST TAIL OF ALL THE DINOSAURS. My neck is made up of 15 bones—see how tall it makes me! My legs are as thick as tree trunks to support my weight.

Draw some trees and plants for me to live in.

73

Grrr!

1 Draw the shape of the skull and add holes for its eye and nose.

2 Add in extra detail including the dinosaur's sharp teeth.

Use shading to make the skull look real.

74

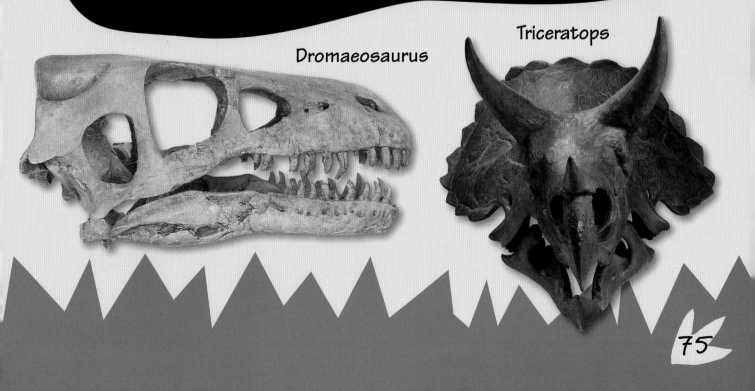

Styracosaurus

Psittacosaurus

Deinonychus

Parasaurolophus

Skulls

LOOK AT THESE SCARY SKULLS to see what dinosaurs were really made of. Try out your drawing skills by sketching the skull of a Dromaeosaurus dinosaur.

Dromaeosaurus

Triceratops

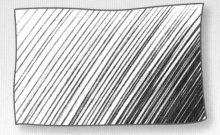

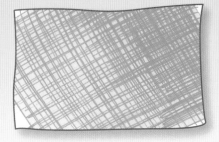

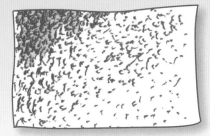

Soft, diagonal lines will add depth to your drawing, but make sure not to press too hard.

For crosshatching, make lots of straight lines close together, then add more going across them. Remember to press lightly.

Stippling means using lots of tiny dots to create shading.

I see!

Try out different pens and pencils to change the look of your dinosaur.

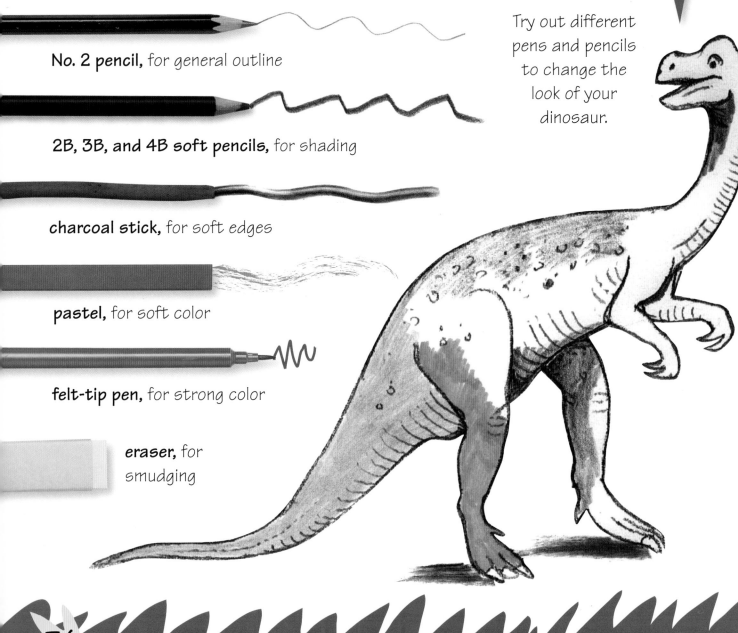

No. 2 pencil, for general outline

2B, 3B, and 4B soft pencils, for shading

charcoal stick, for soft edges

pastel, for soft color

felt-tip pen, for strong color

eraser, for smudging

Compare the two images above to see what a big difference shading can make.

Shading

USE DIFFERENT TYPES OF SHADING to make your drawings look more exciting. Create a 3-D effect with thick lines, big and small dots, and colors.

I'm shady!

Use lots of colors to create a bright pattern on the dinosaur's skin.

Coloring in

HAVE FUN AND GET CREATIVE WHEN YOU COLOR in your dinosaur drawings. See the difference that colored pencils, felt-tip pens, and pastels can make.

Try blending blues, greens, and yellows with your pastels.

Tyrannosaurus rex

Use light and dark colored pencils to make the dinosaur's skin patterned.

Stegosaurus

Struthiomimus

Quick! The dinosaur is running away with the pencil.

Diplodocus

Larger dinosaurs would probably have had drab and dark colors on their skin.

Dromaeosaurus skull

Use yellow and cream felt-tips for the bones and teeth.

I'm positively beaming!

Dinosaurs' skin blended into the background of leaves and trees. Use colored pencils to make a dinosaur's skin green and yellow.

Triceratops

1 Begin with a long curved line and lots of circle shapes.

2 Draw an outline around the circle shapes for the dinosaur's body.

Euoplocephalus

I HAVE A BUILT-IN CLUB AT THE END OF MY TAIL to scare away any enemies. I also have plates sticking out of my skin to protect me against predators. See if you can draw my armor!

3 Add horns, feet, and a tail.

4 Finish your drawing by adding plates to the dinosaur's back.

81

1 Begin with basic shapes for the body and head. Use lines for the legs, arms, and tail.

2 Draw around the shapes for the outline of the dinosaur's body. The line will touch the circles.

Velociraptor

MY CLAWS ARE DEADLY. I use them to attack my prey. You don't want to mess with me so stay out of the way! See how well you can draw my claws and scaly skin.

Gnash!

3 Put detail on the dinosaur's arms and legs.

4 Draw eyes and teeth on your dinosaur. Erase the circles to finish off your drawing.

Draw a pattern on the dinosaur's skin and some landscape for it to live in.

83

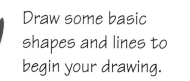

1 Draw some basic shapes and lines to begin your drawing.

2 Draw around the shapes to create the wings, head, and beak.

3 Finish by adding details on the wings and head. Don't forget to draw some clouds too.

Pteranodon

I RULE THE SKIES. Although people often think I'm a dinosaur I am actually part of the reptile family. My wingspan can be up to 30 feet (9 meters). Start drawing my wings so I can fly up into the clouds!

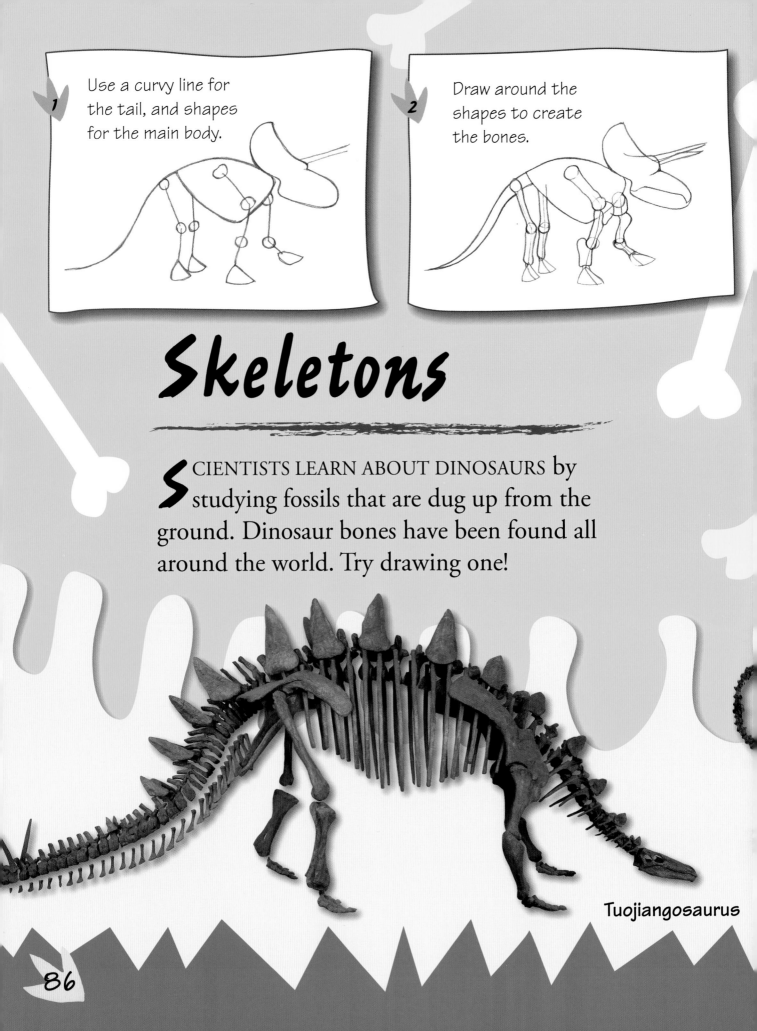

1 Use a curvy line for the tail, and shapes for the main body.

2 Draw around the shapes to create the bones.

Skeletons

SCIENTISTS LEARN ABOUT DINOSAURS by studying fossils that are dug up from the ground. Dinosaur bones have been found all around the world. Try drawing one!

Tuojiangosaurus

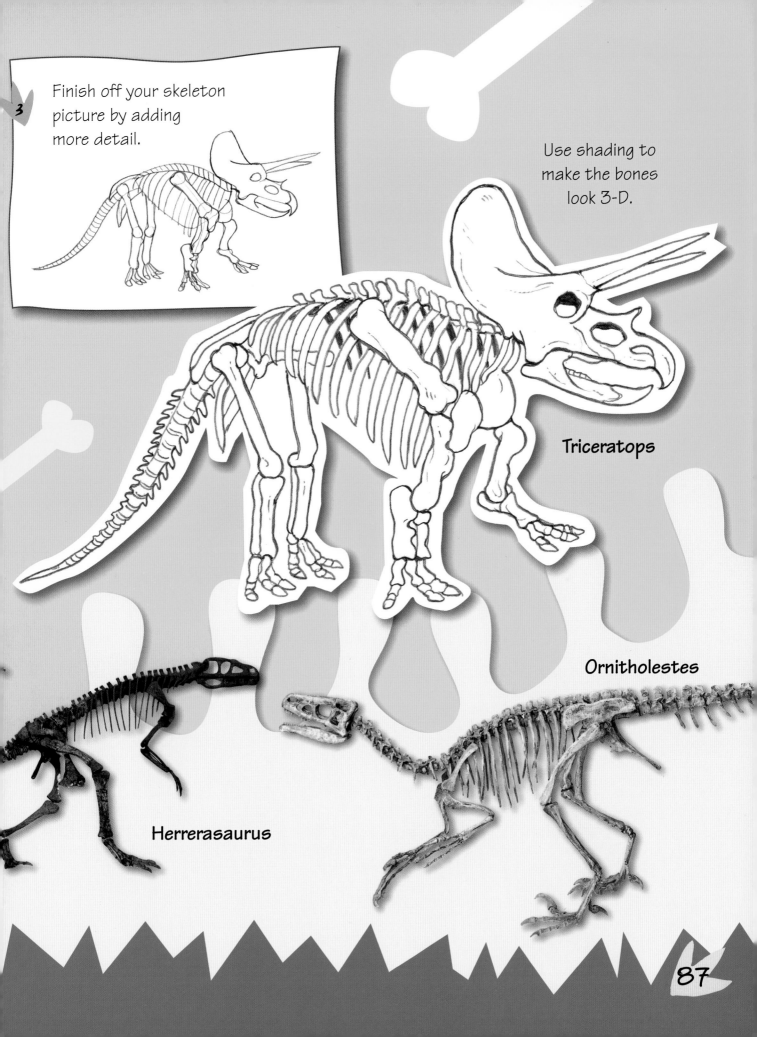

3 Finish off your skeleton picture by adding more detail.

Use shading to make the bones look 3-D.

Triceratops

Ornitholestes

Herrerasaurus

87

Color

NOBODY KNOWS exactly what colors dinosaurs were. Scientists have made guesses by comparing dinosaurs to animals alive today. Patterns and colors on dinosaurs' skin would have helped them hide from enemies.

Red and orange will liven up your pictures of dinosaurs.

Use different shades of blue for feathers and some of the dinosaurs' skin.

Corythosaurus

Compsognathus

Use green and yellow colored pencils to brighten up your drawings.

Giganotosaurus

Feathers

FEATHERS DECORATED SOME DINOSAURS as well as kept them warm. See how well you can copy the textures and colors of the feathers below.

Fancy!

Velociraptor

Archaeopteryx

Look at my pretty feathers!

Archaeopteryx

89

1 Draw a squiggly line for the tail and body shape. Use small and large circles for the head, arms, and legs.

2 When you draw around the circles, the dinosaur begins to take shape.

Corythosaurus

I CAN MAKE SOUNDS THROUGH THE CREST ON MY HEAD. I have three toes on both of my feet, which are strong enough to hold up all of my weight.

Give your dinosaur an eye and decorate the crest on its head with lines.

3

Using shading to make the dinosaur's skin look scaly.

Kerwee!
Kerwoo!

1 Use a circle for the dinosaur's body and an oval for its head. Lines create its neck, tail, and flippers.

2 Draw an outline around the dinosaur's body and flippers. Add one eye.

Elasmosaurus
(Plesiosaur)

I RULE THE SEA, with my great long neck and tail. I swim around happily. I have large eyes so I can see my prey.

92

Complete your drawing by adding the dinosaur's teeth and nose. Use shading on its skin.

93

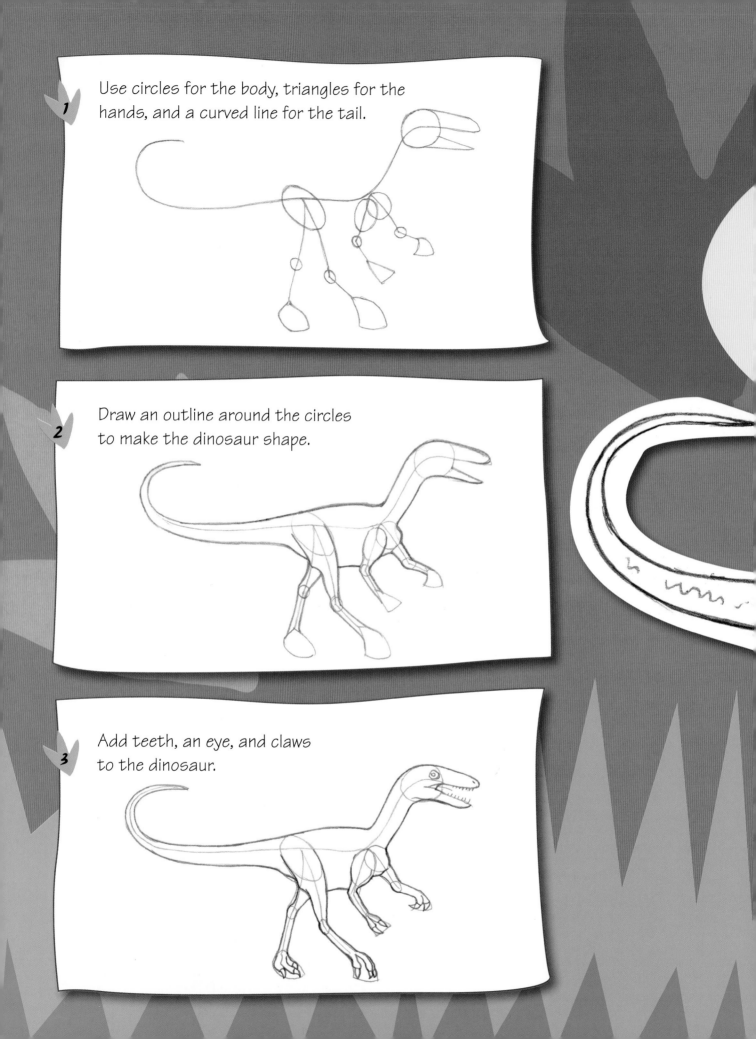

1 Use circles for the body, triangles for the hands, and a curved line for the tail.

2 Draw an outline around the circles to make the dinosaur shape.

3 Add teeth, an eye, and claws to the dinosaur.

Compsognathus

I AM THE SMALLEST DINOSAUR ever to walk the
Earth (no bigger than the size of a chicken).
I like to eat insects and lizards. Try drawing
me next to one of the other dinosaurs,
but don't forget to make me a lot smaller!

Grrr!

Coloring in

When using pastels, smudge the colors together to get a soft effect.

BRING YOUR DINOSAURS TO LIFE by coloring them in. Add finishing touches like grass, plants, and the sky.

Triceratops skeleton

Colored pencils can give your drawing depth.

Pteranodon

Corythosaurus

Make pretty patterns with colored pencils.

Compognathus

Use brightly colored felt-tip pens to decorate your dinosaur.

Use felt-tip pens to draw in surroundings like grass and mud.

Euoplocephalus

Draw over the pencil outline with colored pencils to make the drawing stand out.

Elasmosaurus (Plesiosaur)

Velociraptor

Color in your Elasmosaurus drawing with green and purple pastels.

Scale

IF DINOSAURS WERE ALIVE TODAY some of them would tower above humans and buildings, although a lot of them would be smaller than an elephant!

Size and scale

See how big dinosaurs were when compared with humans. Look at how tall the Tyrannosaurus rex and Corythosaurus were!

Triceratops

Tyrannosaurus rex

Corythosaurus

Pteranodon

Velociraptor

I can draw Machines

Machine stuff

COPY THE TEXTURES YOU SEE on everyday objects to make your drawings look like real machines. Use the equipment shown below to get different effects.

paintbrush

charcoal

soft pencil

No. 2 pencil

felt-tips

oil pastels

water-soluble colored pencils

Color in a drawing with water-soluble colored pencils. Use a wet paintbrush to soften the color and make it look more like paint.

colored pencils

eraser

pencil sharpener

Start drawing in your sketch pad ... try out all the machines in this book

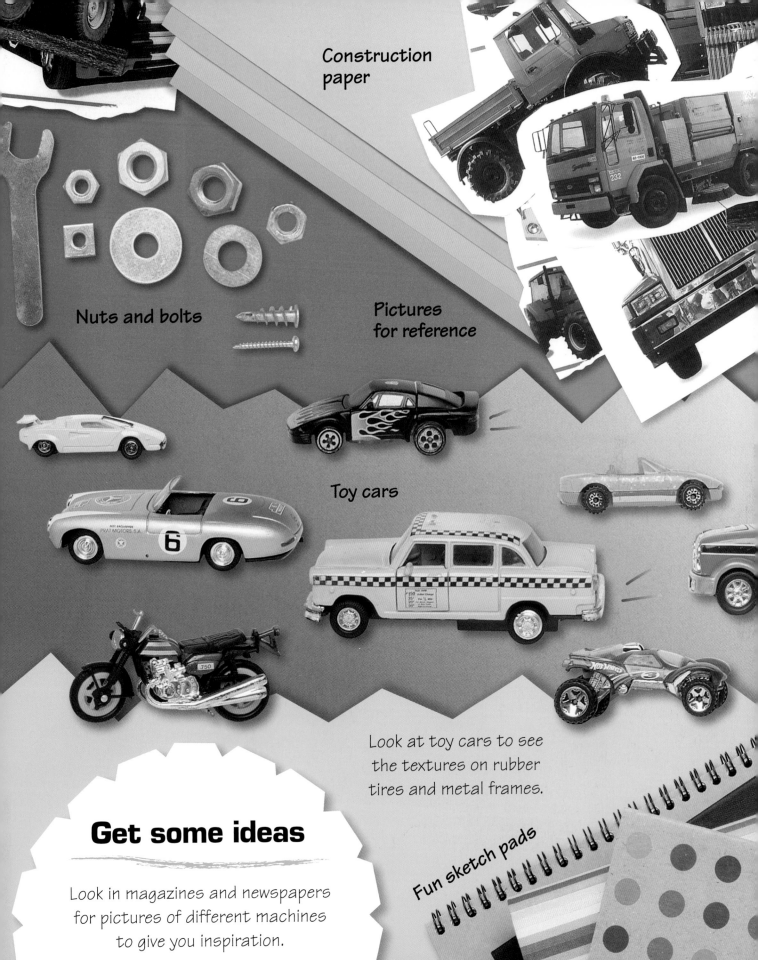

Construction paper

Nuts and bolts

Pictures for reference

Toy cars

Look at toy cars to see the textures on rubber tires and metal frames.

Get some ideas

Look in magazines and newspapers for pictures of different machines to give you inspiration.

Fun sketch pads

Photo gallery

Zip!

High-speed, jet-engine airplane

M ACHINES COME IN A HUGE variety of shapes and sizes. As well as working through the projects in this book, try using the images below for inspiration. That way you can turn out a steam train, a ferry boat, a bicycle, and lots, lots more!

Steam train

1868

Bicycle

Cleeeeeeear the road!

Drag car

TENNECO Automotive · WALKER · MONROE · DYNOMAX Performance Exhaust · RANCHO · Valvoline · Keystr

Autolite · EXIDE · DAYCO · plasti-kote · Ventshade

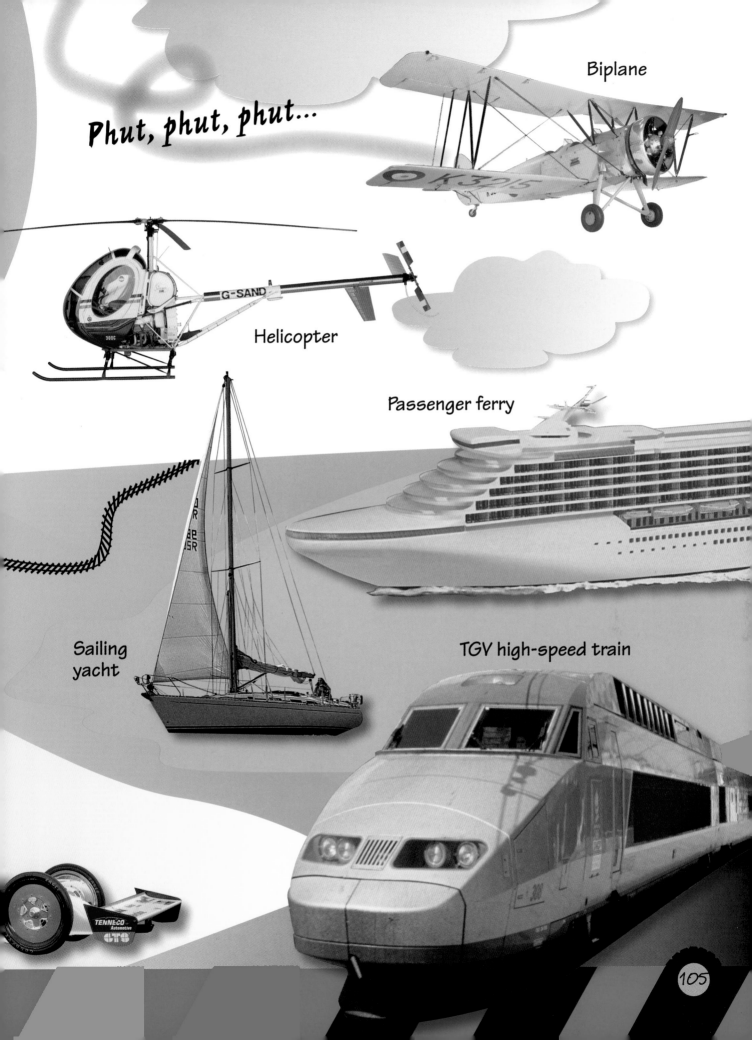

Biplane

Phut, phut, phut...

Helicopter

Passenger ferry

Sailing yacht

TGV high-speed train

1. Make a straight line for your sports car to sit on, then draw two circles the same size for its front and back tIres. Following the drawing below, outline the car's shape.

2. Changing your outline slightly, fill in the shapes of the front of the car, the windows, and the wheel arches.

3. Fill in details such as the door and its handle, the window bars, the seats, and the headlights. Outline the hubcaps on the tIres. Don't forget to erase the circles and lines from step 1.

Sports car

DESIGNED MAINLY TO REACH high speeds and look good, most sports cars are built to travel on ordinary roads (not racetracks). Some are very small, some have very low seats, and many are uncomfortable to ride in, but their owners love them anyway.

Finish by finding a picture of sporty hubcaps that you can copy, to make sure the ones on your sports car are detailed and realistic.

Vrroom!

89

1 Start by drawing a straight line for the road or track your race car will sit on. Now draw a circle at each end, making the one on the right a little smaller. These will be the front and back tires.

2 Join the front of the car to the back tire with a curved line. This will give the front a pointed shape so it cuts through the wind when it's racing. Draw another line above the road to finish the outline.

nee-oowww

5

27

11

3 Sketch in the shape of the cockpit (where the driver sits), then use your eraser to take away the part of the long, curved line above it. Add the roll bar and body details.

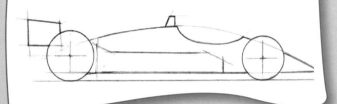

4 Fill in the rearview mirror, the windshield, and the back spoiler, which works in the opposite way from airplane wings—it holds the car down to the ground instead of lifting it up.

Finish by adding the air vents and hubcaps. Remember that the front and back wheels are different!

Race car

SOME CARS ARE BUILT specially to race around a track rather than to take people from place to place. Because their only purpose is to go very fast, they don't look like ordinary cars.

WHEN YOU'VE DRAWN all the cars in this book, look through books and magazines to find inspiration for your automobile art. In the meantime, here are some more cool wheels to be getting on with.

More car ideas

Saab Sonet

Rally car

Alfa Romeo

DE·52·69

Ford sedan

Mini

Beach

Porsche

Honk, honk!

Stretch limousine

Stretch New York

111

1 Using mostly straight lines, draw shapes for the wings, the tail, and the main body of the airplane in the middle of your page.

2 Give the airplane engines using four small, squashed ovals. The plane can't fly without its engines!

3 Draw the cockpit windows, and add some more details to the wings and engines.

4 Keep adding details until you have a finished airplane. You could draw a few clouds at the very top of your page for your airplane to fly through!

Airplane

Up, UP, UP, AND AWAY! Watch the airplane take off from the runway and fly up into the clouds.

Add more details like windows and doors. Use shading on the insides of the engines.

Stealth bomber

DESIGNED SO THAT ENEMIES HAVE TROUBLE DETECTING IT, the stealth bomber is a US military aircraft. It has a wingspan of 172 feet (52 meters) and its engines are inside the plane to muffle the noise they create.

1 Start off with three basic lines drawn at the angles shown below.

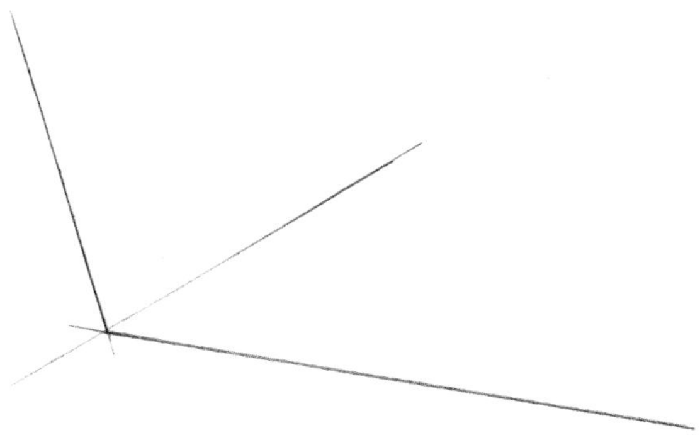

2 Add to these three lines to create your stealth bomber's fuselage (main body), wings, and rudders.

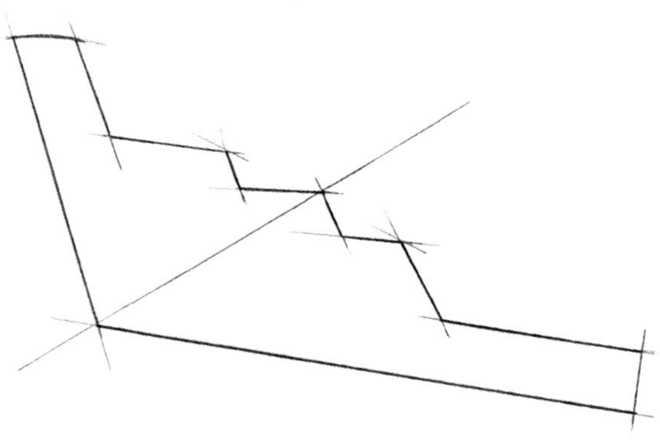

Whooosh!

Use shading to add more interest to your drawing.

③ Draw covers for the engine air vents and a base for the cockpit. Stealth bombers only need a crew of two people.

④ Draw windows on the cockpit and put more details on the wings and back of the plane.

Each commercial airplane is painted in special colors to show which company—or country—owns it. The design includes its logo.

Hide or highlight?

THREE OF THESE MACHINES are painted in bright colors so people will see and recognize them quickly. The fourth machine needs to be almost invisible to do its job. Can you guess which one this is?

Flashy sports cars often have hubcabs that match their shiny paintwork.

colored
pencils

This stealth
bomber is night-
sky blue all over.

Race-car colors let
everyone know who is
sponsoring the team.

11

felt-tips

Shading

ADD INTEREST AND DEPTH to your drawings using shading. Try out the different materials below to create a range of shades in black and gray as well as experimenting with other colors.

pastel, for soft shading

felt-tip pen, for strong flat color

No. 2 pencil, for general outline and solid shading

oil pastel, for heavy color

crayon, for soft shading

eraser, for smudging

2B, 3B, and 4B soft pencils, for shading

Types of shading

Create a range of effects with different shading methods.

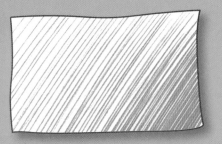

Soft, diagonal lines will add depth to your drawing, but make sure not to press too hard.

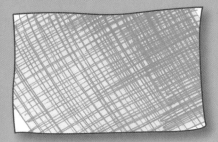

When crosshatching, draw lines in two directions, one over the other, pressing lightly.

For stippling, create shading by using lots of tiny dots.

Look at these drawings of planes. Shading has made the one below more interesting.

Make your plane more exciting and lifelike with exhaust smoke coming out of the engines.

Compare these images (right) to see how shading can make your drawing better.

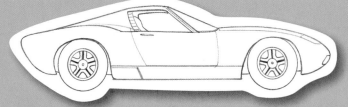

Use smudged lines at the back of the car to make it look as if it's moving.

① To create an outline for your drawing, start with straight lines, rectangles, and half an egg shape, which will become the main bucket.

② Give the bucket its shape, draw in metal crawler tracks, and add more lines on the huge arm that controls the backhoe.

Backhoe

THESE MONSTER MACHINES are used in mines and quarries. Their teeth can cut away at solid rock and move thousands of tons of dirt or stone every day. One of these backhoes weighs about 24 times as much as a really big truck.

3 Keep adding detail to the bucket, the arm, the bottom of the backhoe, and the tracks, then sketch in the windows of the driver's cab.

4 Fill in the cab roof, the high access ladder, and the main body of the machine, where the engine lives.

Use fine lines and shading to fill the bucket with rocks, and make the tubes, nuts, tracks, and ground surface look realistic.

CRRRunch

1 The framework of a roller is made up of lots of simple lines and shapes like a plastic toy. Use circles, cylinders, squares, and rectangles to start with.

2 Even the basic details take the form of straight lines and simple curves. Create the bars around the wheels, for example, with parallel lines and half circles.

3 Draw the cab windows and window bars, and the body markings. Try using a little shading to make some details—such as tires and bars—look 3-D.

Roller

USED TO LAY hard surfaces, rollers have three huge wheels, which are actually drums filled with water. They press down on the tar-and-stone surface of a new road to make it smooth and flat.

Chugg, chugg

Finish with more shading and extra detail on the drum wheels and the body.

1 Begin by outlining the dumptruck's body, the lifting machine underneath, and its two huge wheels— each one of them is taller than a horse!

2 Now add the cab, where the driver sits, give more shape to the truck, and draw some lines to show the shape of the truck bed.

3 The driver's cab door and windows come next, as well as one of the sliding arms, or pistons, that lift the bed to dump its load.

Dumptruck

CRASH, BANG, SCRAPE! Here comes a dumptruck full of dirt and rocks from a huge construction site or a mine. This truck is more than twice as tall as a grown man.

Vrroom!

Finish by drawing in all the tire details, filling the body with a mound of rubble, and sketching a stony surface for your dumptruck to drive on.

125

Tractor

TRACTORS ARE THE MOST IMPORTANT machines on farms. Their powerful engines can pull other heavy machines that do different jobs, like harvesting crops.

① Use lines for the main body of the tractor, a large circle for the back wheel, and a smaller circle for the front wheel.

② Give your tractor a door, windows, and a roof. Draw smaller circles inside both wheels.

Erase any pencil lines that you don't need and firm up final lines with a pen or dark pencil.

3 Draw even smaller circles inside the wheels. Add some steps, a steering wheel, and a long pipe.

4 Put ridges on the tires for grip in muddy fields. Add finishing details to the rest of the tractor.

felt-tips

A dumptruck's load can
weigh as much as 18 elephants.
Try to stay out of its way!

Big rollers are
meant to flatten
new roads, so they
are very heavy.

oil pastels

pastels

Look out!

colored pencils

Big backhoes scoop up tons of soil and rock—if you get in the way, they might scoop you up too!

HEAVY MACHINES DO the hard work on farms and construction sites. But because they're powerful, they're very dangerous. They're bright colors so people can see them coming.

Tractors have to be very heavy to pull other farm machines.

felt-tips

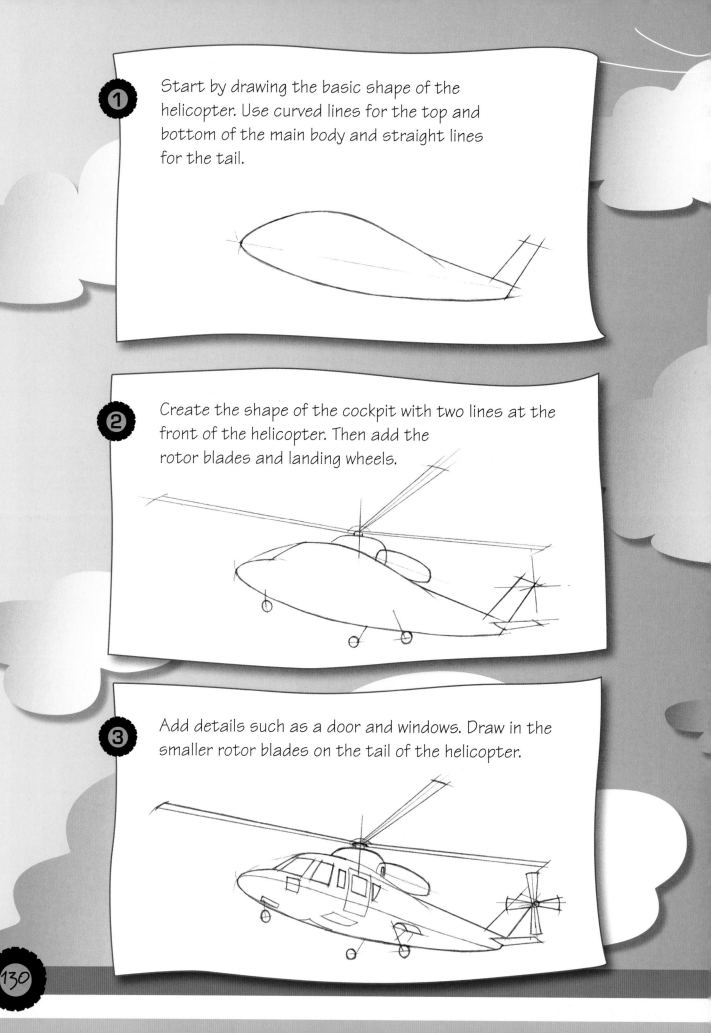

1 Start by drawing the basic shape of the helicopter. Use curved lines for the top and bottom of the main body and straight lines for the tail.

2 Create the shape of the cockpit with two lines at the front of the helicopter. Then add the rotor blades and landing wheels.

3 Add details such as a door and windows. Draw in the smaller rotor blades on the tail of the helicopter.

Whirrrrr

Helicopter

SUITABLE FOR LANDING AND TAKING OFF IN SMALL SPACES, helicopters are incredibly useful. In addition to carrying people around, they get involved in sea and land rescue, firefighting, military operations, and traffic control.

A helicopter has two sets of rotor blades—a big one on top and a small one at the back.

1 Draw two lines that meet toward the corner of your paper, so the train will look as if it's disappearing into the distance. Now outline the train with its rounded nose and slanted front.

2 Add the driver's window lines, separating the nose and the roof from the body, and a few sets of wheels peeking out underneath the carriage.

3 Fill in the headlights on the front, the passenger doors and windows, and the shape of the tracks underneath.

Whoooosh

High-speed train

HERE COMES A HIGH-SPEED train, carrying lots and lots of people very, very fast. These trains run on electricity—some of them get their power from an overhead cable, and some get it from one of their tracks.

Texture

YOU CAN FIND LOTS OF DIFFERENT TEXTURES on machines. Some machine parts are smooth and shiny (car hoods and doors), whereas other areas are rough and bumpy (car tires).

eraser, for smudging

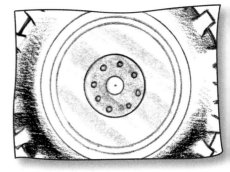

Use a light blue charcoal to make the metal on the tractor wheel look shiny.

oil pastel, for blending colors

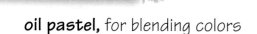

4B soft pencils are thicker than 2B and 3B. Use the right thickness to get the effect you want.

2B, 3B, and 4B soft pencils, for shading

charcoal stick, for blurred edges

soft pastel, also for blending

Vintage car

See how shiny the hood and bumper are. Copy the straight lines and shine on the grille.

Words to get you going

bumpy
rubber tracks
shiny metal
rough GRITTY
smooth

Get the ridges on your tires to look 3-D with shading. Charcoal or soft pencils are perfect for making a rough texture.

Tractor tires

A backhoe's caterpillar tracks

Make an even-looking finish for tire surfaces using 2B, 3B, and 4B soft pencils.

Car wheel

Dump-truck wheels

Tires and tracks

Grooves and ridges in tractor tires and backhoe caterpillar tracks give the vehicles grip on slippery mud. Re-create the look of grooves and ridges on your drawings.

A No. 2 pencil is good for drawing thin lines and for shading in areas on the tracks.

1 Start by drawing the bike's basic shape. Remember that the wheels are fairly big compared with the body.

2 Fill in the curved shapes of the frame, the windshield, the seat, and the wheel rims. If necessary, pencil in straight lines to guide you, then erase them later on.

3 Add more details on the body, and important elements such as the handlebars, exhaust, footrest, and the tire guard.

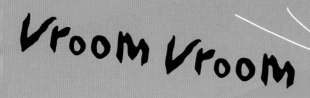

Vroom Vroom

Motorcycle

CONTROLLED USING HANDLEBARS instead of a steering wheel, motorcycles have powerful engines, but only two wheels. Sports bikes like this one can reach high speeds very quickly, and take sharp corners with no problem at all.

Finish with realistic touches like air vents metalwork, rivets, and subtle shading.

1 Use two long curved lines and one short one to form the speedboat's basic shape. Its frame (called the hull) is pointed at the front so it can cut through water easily.

2 Add squiggly lines to look like the water's surface, and a boxy shape on top of the boat for the windshield.

3 Add detailing to the hull and windshield, and a few rippling waves, and sketch the driver in his high-backed seat.

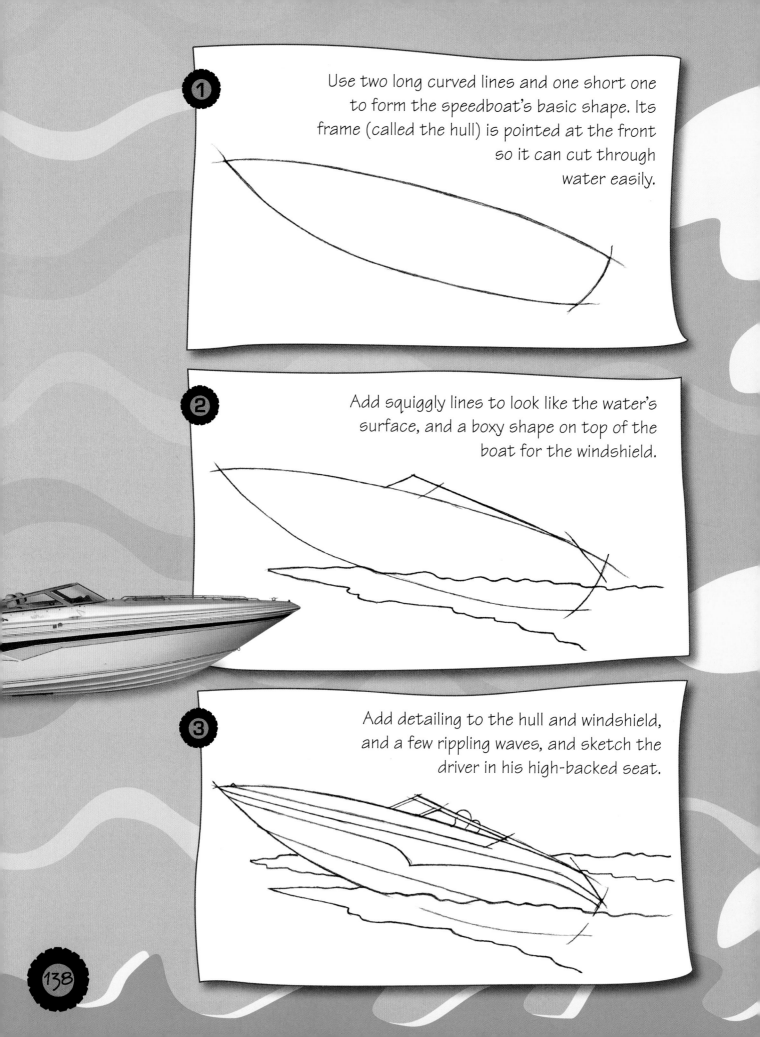

Speedboat

THIS SMALL, POWERFUL boat bounces through the waves at high speed. It is used in racing, for towing water skiers, as a patrol boat, and just for fun!

Zoooom!

A little shading and some extra detailing on the hull will bring your speedboat to life.

1 Start with circles and curved lines for the wheels. Straight lines form the main body of the truck.

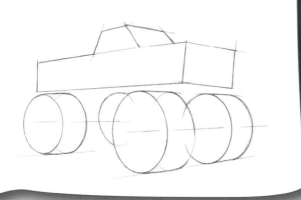

2 Draw smaller circles inside the wheels, curved wheel arches, a light on top of the roof, and a front grille.

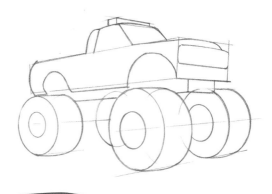

Monster truck

MONSTER TRUCKS are built from pick-up trucks or van bodies. Each one is slightly different. They entertain crowds at large shows by running over cars with their huge wheels and crushing them.

3 Add a rearview mirror, a door, suspension bars, headlights, lines on the grille, and detail on the wheels.

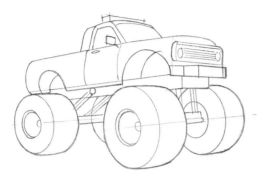

4 Give your monster truck some flags and draw the V-shaped tread on the tires.

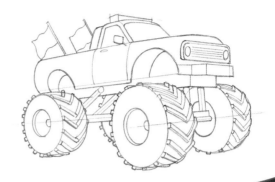

Vrrr-ramm!

Helicopters are used to fight fires, rescue people and take them to the hospital.

pastel

oil pastels

Monster strucks put on a fantastic show.

felt-tips

High-speed trains whizz people over long distances.

colored pencils

Watch me!

SOME MACHINES ARE REALLY fun to watch, and their jazzy paintwork makes them even more exciting.

Speedboats cut through the water, but it's still a bumpy ride.

Motorcycles make sleek racers.

pastels

oil pastels

Scale

MOST MACHINES ARE TALLER THAN YOU, especially monster trucks! Race cars are relatively small in scale compared to other vehicles like backhoes and jumbo jets. If they were too big and bulky they wouldn't win the race!

The largest monster trucks are 13 feet (4 meters) tall. Each tire is over 5.5 feet (1.65 meters) high—that's taller than a normal car.

The tailfin on a jumbo jet is 65 feet (20 meters) high, which is as tall as a six-story building!

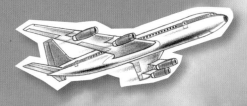

Airplanes and helicopters look tiny up in the sky, but when you see them close up they tower above you.

The giant backhoe needs to be big in order to do its job. It can fill a giant dumptruck in minutes.

I can draw
Magical
Creatures

Magic stuff

CREATE YOUR OWN MAGIC with the tools below. Bring your drawings to life with colors and shading.

Oil pastels for coloring in your drawings.

Soft pastels can create a gentle look which is good for fairies and princesses.

No. 2 pencil

4B soft pencil

charcoal

For shading effects, use an eraser or your finger to smudge soft pastels and charcoal.

colored pencils

sketch pad

colored paper

pencil sharpener

Color in a drawing with water-soluble colored pencils. Use a wet paintbrush to soften the color and make it look more like paint.

References

Stuck for ideas? Take a look around you and see what inspiration you can get from toys, magazines, and newspapers.

feathers

pictures from magazines, postcards, and books

felt-tip pen for strong color

ballpoint pen for strong outlines

toy figures and puppets for reference

jewels

1 Use a large oval for the fairy's head, and smaller circles for her joints, hands, and feet. Lines make up her arms and legs.

2 Give the fairy wings and a wand. Draw in her hands, arms, and legs.

Flower fairy

I AM A FLOWER FAIRY, see how I flutter my wings. I am as pretty as a petal. I sprinkle magical fairy dust with my wand.

3 Add eyes, hair, a mouth, and a nose. Decorate your fairy with a pretty dress and striped stockings.

Use shading to decorate your fairy's dress.

1 Start with some circles and lines.

2 Draw arms, hands, wings, feet, and legs.

3 Draw in your ballerina's face, hair, and dress.

Ballerina fairy

HERE IS THE LOVELY dancing fairy, so light on her toes. Make her dance around your page.

1 Use lines as the basis of your fairy's arms and legs. Circle and oval shapes make up the feet, hands, and head.

2 Give your fairy wings, legs, arms, a hand, and a tooth to hold.

3 Draw hair, eyes, a nose, and a mouth. Give your fairy a pretty dress to wear.

Use shading
and stippling
to decorate
your fairy's
hair and dress.

Tooth fairy

DREAM OF TWINKLY STARS,
as your very own Tooth
fairy comes to swap your tooth
for some money!

Zzzzz

Taddaaaa!

Fairy faces

Your PENCILS, PENS, AND PASTELS are like magic wands. Use them to make your fairies look beautiful!

Try some smaller flowers for your fairy's crown.

Fairy headwear

There are plenty of ways to dress up your fairies. Create amazing headwear for them to fly around in.

Here's an interesting design!

Make a pretty hat that looks like one big flower.

Fairy hairstyles

Be creative with your drawings and give your fairies some fun hairdos. You're the one with the pencil so you can decide what to try out; short and curly or long and wavy!

This fairy's hairstyle is fun and easy to draw.

Decorate your fairy's hair with a ribbon and give her a necklace to wear.

Draw thick and wavy hair using curved lines and shading.

To get this unusual hairstyle use lots of spirals in a pile on top of her head.

Fairytastic

1 Begin with circles and lines for your mermaid's upper body; add curved lines for her tail.

2 Draw in her fingers, two shells, a belly button, and an outline for her neck and arms.

3 Give your mermaid eyes, hair, a mouth, and a nose. Put scales on her tail.

Mermaid

"ILOVE TO SPLASH AROUND IN THE WAVES and swim with the fish. I visit the shore every now and then, but I live in the sea since I can't stay out of the water for too long!"

Magical colors

HAVE FUN AND GET CREATIVE when coloring in your magical creatures. See the amazing difference that pastels, water-soluble colored pencils, and felt-tip pens can make!

Witch

Color in your witch's hair, dress, and shoes with colored pencils. Don't make her dress a solid black; use shading to make it lighter in some areas. Create a rough texture on her hair and broomstick using oil pastels.

Wizard

Using felt-tip pens, make your wizard's cloak look like velvet. He is a wise and old wizard so keep his hair and beard white.

Flower Fairy

This flower fairy has been colored in with soft pastels. Use two colors and blend them together.

Before you get going try out some different combinations of colors and materials on the side of the page.

Mermaid

Color in your pretty mermaid with water-soluble colored pencils.

Elf

Use colored pencils to decorate your elf. Try different shades of green for his hat and shirt. Add depth to your drawing by shading his bag and scarf to make them look worn.

Princess

MEET THE PRETTY PRINCESS. She looks sweet in her patterned dress. She lives in a magical kingdom. If she kisses the frog he might turn into a prince!

ribbit!

1 — Begin with basic shapes and lines for your drawing.

2 — Make an outline for her dress, arms, neck, and shoes.

Use shading and coloring to dress up your princess!

3
Draw her hair, eyes, mouth and nose. Add a crown, hearts on her dress, and a frog for her to hold.

Basic shapes and lines make up the main body parts for the prince.

Draw an outline around the prince's body. Give him a cloak and clothes.

Prince

Draw a royal prince who is ready to rule a kingdom, fight a dragon, and charm a princess. In order to look the part he needs a crown, a sword, and a stylish cloak.

3 Put hair and a crown on the prince's head. Draw in his face and give him a belt and sword.

colored pencils

Use colored pencils as well as 2B, 3B, 4B, and No. 2 pencils to build up hatching.

oil pastels

Oil pastels can also create shadows—try using two shades of the same color.

felt-tips

Use different shades of colored felt-tips to create strong effects.

soft pastels

soft pastels create soft effects

Charcoal is especially good for soft shadows on the ground.

charcoal

eraser

Types of shading

Soft, diagonal lines will add depth to your drawing, but make sure not to press too hard.

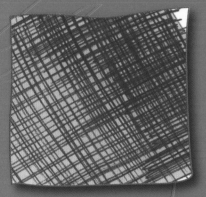

When crosshatching, draw lines in two directions, one over the other, pressing lightly.

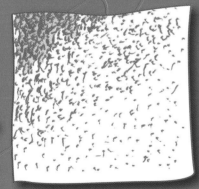

In stippling, shading is created by using lots of tiny dots.

Shading

He looks a bit shady...

CREATE A 3-D EFFECT on your drawings with clever shading. Make your dragons and witches look more scary, and your princess and prince more important by using areas of light and dark.

Shady wings

See how these wings have been improved with dark and light shading.

1 Start with cirles in different sizes for the unicorn's head, body, and leg joints.

2 Draw an outline for the body. Give it a tail, ears, and a horn. Draw two curved lines for its wings.

3 Finish the wing with lots of curved lines in a row. Give the unicorn a mane, eyes, a mouth, and nose. Decorate its horn.

Unicorn

A UNICORN IS A MYTHICAL CREATURE with magical powers. It looks like a horse, but one with wings and a horn coming out of its forehead.

Use shading to make your drawing look more interesting.

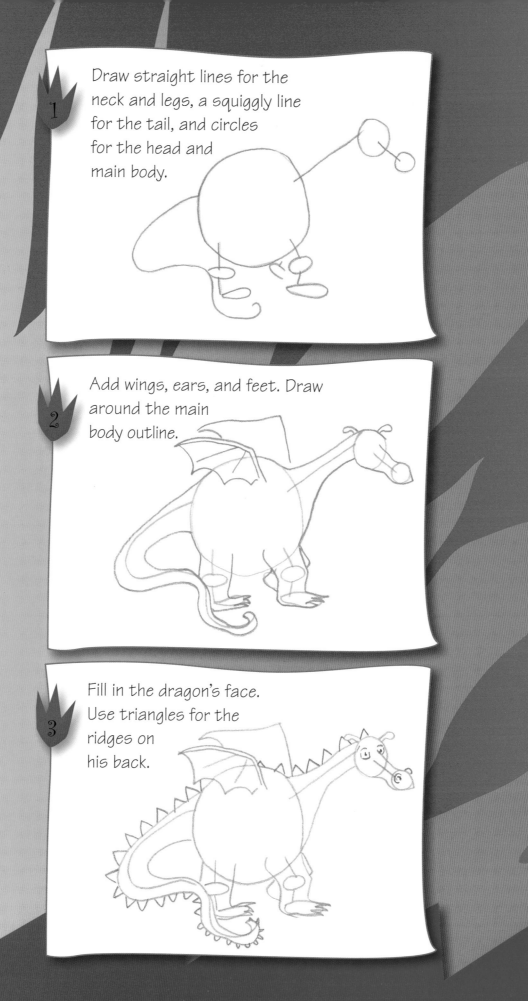

1 Draw straight lines for the neck and legs, a squiggly line for the tail, and circles for the head and main body.

2 Add wings, ears, and feet. Draw around the main body outline.

3 Fill in the dragon's face. Use triangles for the ridges on his back.

Dragon

LEGENDS FROM DIFFERENT COUNTRIES describe dragons as large fire-breathing reptiles with wings. Dragons were seen as terrifying creatures that often guarded treasure or maidens.

Puff!

Use shading on the dragon's body to make him look more lifelike.

1 Draw circles, semicircles, squiggly lines, and a triangle.

2 Create an outline around the dragon's body, head, and tail. Give him wings!

1 Begin with basic shapes and curved lines.

2 Draw around the shapes to make your dragon.

Draw eyes, a mouth, and nose. Use shading on his wings.

More dragons

I**N FAIRY TALES PEOPLE** were terrified of dragons because they were thought to fly and breathe fire. Princes were sent off to kill dragons in order to protect people—and rescue princesses.

Use shading on his skin and draw lines on the front of his belly and neck.

1 Draw a large circle for the elf's head, and lines for his legs and arms. Use basic shapes for his body, feet, and joints.

2 Give your elf shorts and a T-shirt to wear. Draw an outline around his arms, hands, and legs.

Elf

ELVES ARE A TYPE OF FAIRY that are popular in myths. These tiny people are said to be friendly to humans, although sometimes they can misbehave! Santa Claus has elves working for him as his helpers.

3 Add in his eyes, mouth, ears, and nose. Draw a hat and a bag. Dress him in striped tights and shoes.

Use shading on your elf's tights, scarf, and bag.

Elf parade

Have fun drawing the elves on their parade. Do you think they are on their way to Santa's workshop?

Once you've drawn some elves try drawing lots of trees and snow!

Bearded elf

Friendly elves

Begin with basic shapes and lines, then give clothes, shoes, and bags to the elves.

1

2

Copy the shapes and lines in step 1. Draw an outline for the elf's body.

1

2

Friendly elf

Draw me a hat!

Use different colors and shading techniques to decorate your drawings.

Helpful elf

Follow the circles and lines in step 1, then give your drawing more details.

1

2

Start with shapes and lines, then give the elf a big nose, clothes, and an apple to hold.

1

2

1 Start with basic shapes for the main parts of the wizard's body and lines for his legs, arms, and neck.

2 Draw a hat and a magical wand. Dress your wizard in a long gown.

Wizard

W ATCH THE WIZARD as he waves his star-shaped wand to perform magical spells and tricks. He is powerful and his name means "wise man." The most famous wizard was named Merlin. Have you heard of him?

3 Give him some hair and a beard. Fill in his face with big eyebrows, a nose, and mouth.

Decorate his gown with yellow stars and moons. Use shading on his hat and gown to make them look real.

Expressions

"MIRROR, MIRROR, ON THE WALL, who is the fairest of them all?" Try drawing different expressions on your magical creatures' faces.

Sad fairy

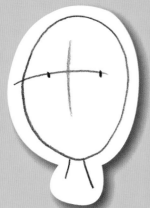

Draw the fairy's head, neck, and eyes.

Add a nose, mouth, and teardrops.

Give her wings, hair, and a crown.

Happy witch

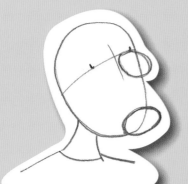

Draw the witch's head, neck, shoulders, and eyes.

Draw her nose with a wart, her hair, mouth, and chin.

Shade in her hair and draw a hat.

Angry goblin

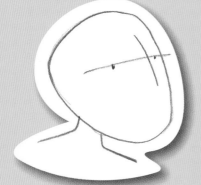

Use two crossed lines to draw eyes in the right place.

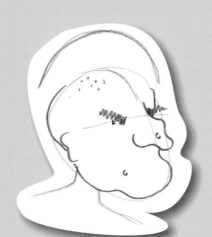

Draw his jawline, eyebrows, nose, and an ear.

Draw his hair and shade it in. Put stubble on his chin.

Tired giant

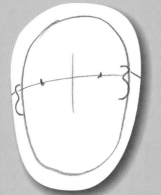

Draw the giant's head, eyes, and ears.

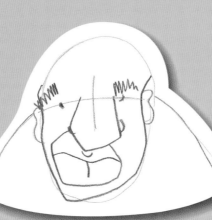

Put in detail on his face and give him shoulders.

Shade in his lips and hair.

Surprised elf

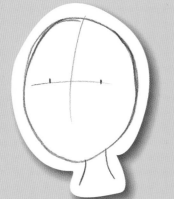

Start by drawing the elf's head, neck, and eyes.

Add a nose, mouth, ears, and eyebrows.

Draw a hat and shade in his eyebrows and mouth.

181

1 Start with circles and basic shapes for the witch's body and broom.

2 Give your witch a hat, arms, hands, and cloak. Draw a cat sitting on her broom.

3 Draw a nose, mouth, and eyes on the witch and her cat. Give the witch some hair.

cackle!
cackle!

Witch

Hubble bubble, here comes trouble... watch out for the flying witch and her cat. Stay away from her cauldron!

1 Begin with basic lines and shapes for the giant's head, body, legs, and arms.

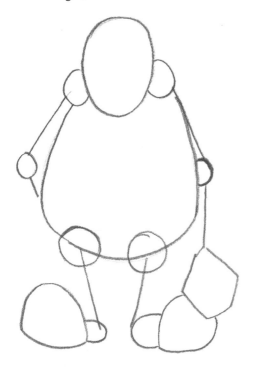

2 Draw around the shapes and lines to create the arms, body, fingers, and legs.

Giant

"FEE, FI, FO, FUM! I smell the blood of an Englishman. You had better stay away from my hen that lays solid-gold eggs, or I won't be a happy, friendly giant!"

3 Give the giant some hair, eyes, a nose, and mouth. Draw his shoes and clothes.

fee, fi, fo, fum...

Texture

MAGICAL CREATURES have a range of textures, from feathery wings on fairies to shiny scales on dragons. Try out different materials to make your magical creatures look lifelike.

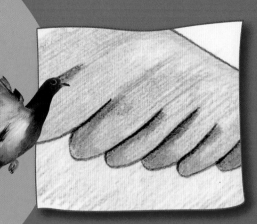

Wings need long, soft pencil strokes to make the feathers soft and light.

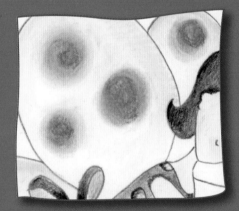

Use a soft pencil or pastel to make fairy wings look light and delicate.

Words to think about

scaly furry bumpy

lumpy smooth slimy

hairy prickly spiky

feathery shiny

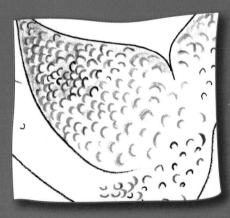

Mermaid tails and bodies have overlapping scales that have a texture like fish skin.

Textures in nature

Look around you (in your home, outside, and in books) to get ideas for adding more texture to your drawings. Can you guess where each texture is from?

This flowery texture would make a delicate fairy wing.

Ssscales are ssso sssuper

Look at these shimmery scales.

A unicorn could fly away with these feathers.

These lumps and bumps are like a witch's warty nose.

Dragons' wings can stretch like this.

Copy this texture to create a fairy's fluttery wings.

Could this be a dragon's scaly skin?

187

troll's
nose boil

runny nose

Body parts

MAGICAL CREATURES ARE
ALL UNIQUE. Have fun
drawing all their body parts!
Once you have tried all the
characters in this book use this
page to give you more ideas.

monster

witch

Hands

Use shading around the
witch's and giant's warts.
Give the witch pointed
fingernails and the
princess pretty pink ones!

goblin

beak

pixie

Noses

Be creative when
drawing and
coloring in noses
on your magical
creatures!

giant

188

troll

dragon

gnome

dragon

Wings

Draw wings with all kinds of textures and shapes.

Feet and claws

Use lots of different colors for the feet and claws on your magical creatures.

Tails

Magical creatures' tails are not at all alike. The mermaid's is slippery and scaly, the dinosaur's is spiked and sharp, and the unicorn's is wispy and wiry.

dragon

fairy

unicorn

mermaid

unicorn

Scale

MAGICAL CREATURES are very different in size. There are tiny fairies and gigantic giants. Be creative and try drawing a few magical creatures on one page. Make sure you keep them to scale.

We're only little

Tiny fairies

Fairies are usually very small. Have fun comparing your drawings to real-life objects to see the difference in size.

Hmmm... I think I prefer the frog

Silly sizes

Fee fi fo fum?

You can play around by changing the scale of different creatures around to make some funny pictures. This giant isn't so big now that he's standing by an oversized elf!

Life-size

Some magical creatures should be drawn to look life-size, such as the prince, princess, and unicorn.

Fly away

The witch looks like she is farther away because she is smaller than the flying dragon.

Any size

Some magical creatures come in many shapes and sizes. Dragons can be big and scary or small and sweet. Try drawing both!

Where's the beach?

Index

Acknowledgements

Dorling Kindersley would like to thank: Marie Bernadette Greenwood for editorial support; Leah Germann, Karen Hood, Tory Gordon-Harris and Jane Bull for design inspiration; Rose Horridge and Claire Bowers for picture research; Zahavit Shalev and Fleur Star for editorial assistance.

Picture credits t = top b = bottom c= center l = left r = right

Peter Anderson © DK 105tr. Roby Braun 99br. Brian Cosgrove 84tl & br, 85b. Brian Cosgrove © DK (background image 144-5). Andy Crawford © DK 102tlb, 105tl (Courtesy of Airport); 106tr; 111tc; 116-17; 118-19; 128-9; 134tr; cl, cla, clb; 137tr; 142-3. Mike Dunning © DK, Courtesy of the National Railway Museum 104c; 133tr. Lynton Gardiner © DK 112tl. Philip Gatwood © DK 104bcr. Steve Gorton © DK 105c. Graham High Centaur Studios – model maker 58cla, 64bl, 65tr, 68tr, 82bl, 98br, 99bl. Alan Keohane © DK 111b. © DK Courtesy of Brookes and Vernons/JCB. © DK, Courtesy of Princess Cruises 105cr. © DK (Courtesy of Goodwood Festival of Speed) 108br; 109bl. Dave King 108cb; 110b; © DK, Courtesy of the National Motor Museum, Beaulieu 135cl. Richard Leeney © DK 101cl; 103tr; 103crb; 104b; 107tl; 120c; 125tr; 126cr; 135c, tc; 140bl; 145cr. Bill Ling © DK 11bc. Chris Mattison © DK 11cl. Eric Meacher © DK 104bl-105br.

Jane Miller © DK 11tr. © Judith Miller / DK / The Design Gallery 180tr. Ray Moller © DK, Penton Hook Marine Sales, Surrey 138cl. NASA 104tl. Gary Ombler © DK 114tl; 136bl. Tim Ridley © DK 111cb. Dave Rudkin 109tr; 111tr. Richard Shellabear © DK, Courtesy of the HET National Automobile Museum, Holland 110cl; 134bl. Graham Staab – model maker 68tl. Chris Stevens 131bl. Matthew Ward © DK 107tr; 110tr; 111c.

Picture montage on top right of page 11: Paul Bricknell © DK 11br. John Daniels © DK 11cr. Christopher & Sally Gable © DK 11t. David Handley © DK 11c. Jacqui Hurst © DK 11bl.

Picture montage on bottom right of page 57: Andy Crawford © DK, courtesy of the Royal Tyrrell Museum of Palaeontology, Alberta, Canada 57t, bl. Sandie Hill © DK 57cl. Ed Homonylo © DK, courtesy of Dinosaur State Park, Connecticut, USA 57b. Colin Keates © DK, courtesy of the Natural History Museum, London 57br. Dave King/Graham High at Centaur Studios – model maker © DK 57cr, tr. Peter Wilson © DK 57tl.

All other images © Dorling Kindersley www.dkimages.com